© THE BAKER & TAYLOR CO.

FIFTY YEARS & OTHER POEMS

AMS PRESS
NEW YORK

FIFTY YEARS & OTHER POEMS

BY

JAMES WELDON JOHNSON

AUTHOR OF

"THE AUTOBIOGRAPHY OF AN EX-COLORED MAN," ETC.

With an Introduction by

BRANDER MATTHEWS

THE CORNHILL COMPANY
BOSTON
1917

Library of Congress Cataloging in Publication Data

Johnson, James Weldon, 1871-1938.
    Fifty years & other poems.

    Reprint of the 1917 ed. published by Cornhill Co.,
Boston.
    I. Title.
PS3519.02625F5   1975   811'.5'2   73-18587
ISBN 0-404-11398-2

From the edition of 1917, Boston
First AMS edition published in 1975
Manufactured in the United States of America

AMS PRESS INC.
NEW YORK, N.Y. 10003

To
G. N. J.

ACKNOWLEDGMENT

FOR permission to reprint certain poems in this book thanks are due to the editors and proprietors of the *Century Magazine*, the *Independent*, *The Crisis*, *The New York Times*, and the following copyright holders, G. Ricordi and Company, G. Schirmer and Company, and Joseph W. Stern and Company.

CONTENTS

CONTENTS

JINGLES & CROONS

INTRODUCTION

OF THE hundred millions who make up the population of the United States ten millions come from a stock ethnically alien to the other ninety millions. They are not descended from ancestors who came here voluntarily, in the spirit of adventure to better themselves or in the spirit of devotion to make sure of freedom to worship God in their own way. They are the grandchildren of men and women brought here against their wills to serve as slaves. It is only half-a-century since they received their freedom and since they were at last permitted to own themselves. They are now American citizens, with the rights and the duties of other American citizens; and they know no language, no literature and no law other than those of their fellow citizens of Anglo-Saxon ancestry.

When we take stock of ourselves these ten millions cannot be left out of account. Yet they are not as we are; they stand apart, more or less; they have their own distinct characteristics. It behooves us to understand them as best we can and to discover what manner of people they are. And we are justified in inquiring how far they have revealed themselves, their racial characteristics, their abiding traits, their longing aspirations, — how far have they disclosed these in one or another of the several arts. They have had their poets, their painters, their composers, and yet most of these have ignored their racial opportunity and have worked in imitation and in emulation of their white predecessors and contemporaries, content to handle again the traditional themes. The most important and the most significant contributions they have made to art are in music, — first in the plaintive beauty of the so-called " Negro spirituals " — and, secondly, in the syncopated melody of so-called " ragtime " which has now taken the whole world captive.

In poetry, especially in the lyric, wherein the soul is free to find full expression for its innermost emotions, their attempts have been, for the most part, divisible into two classes. In the first of these may be grouped the verses in which the lyrist put forth sentiments common to all mankind and in no wise specifically those of his own race; and from the days of Phyllis Wheatley to the present the most of the poems written by men who were not wholly white are indistinguishable from the poems written by men who were wholly white. Whatever their merits might be, these verses cast

little or no light upon the deeper racial senti-
ments of the people to whom the poets them-
selves belonged. But in the lyrics to be grouped
in the second of these classes there was a racial
quality. This contained the dialect verses in
which there was an avowed purpose of recaptur-
ing the color, the flavor, the movement of life
in " the quarters," in the cotton field and in the
canebrake. Even in this effort, white authors
had led the way; Irvin Russell and Joel Chand-
ler Harris had made the path straight for Paul
Laurence Dunbar, with his lilting lyrics, often
infused with the pathos of a down-trodden folk.

In the following pages Mr. James Weldon
Johnson conforms to both of these traditions.
He gathers together a group of lyrics, delicate
in workmanship, fragrant with sentiment, and
phrased in pure and unexceptionable English.
Then he has another group of dialect verses,
racy of the soil, pungent in flavor, swinging in
rhythm and adroit in rhyme. But where he
shows himself a pioneer is the half-dozen larger
and bolder poems, of a loftier strain, in which
he has been nobly successful in expressing
the higher aspirations of his own people. It
is in uttering this cry for recognition, for sym-
pathy, for understanding, and above all, for
justice, that Mr. Johnson is most original and
most powerful. In the superb and soaring

INTRODUCTION

stanzas of " Fifty Years " (published exactly
half-a-century after the signing of the Emanci-
pation Proclamation) he has given us one of
the noblest commemorative poems yet written
by any American, — a poem sonorous in its
diction, vigorous in its workmanship, elevated
in its imagination and sincere in its emotion.
In it speaks the voice of his race; and the race
is fortunate in its spokesman. In it a fine theme
has been finely treated. In it we are made to
see something of the soul of the people who are
our fellow citizens now and forever, — even if
we do not always so regard them. In it we
are glad to acclaim a poem which any living
poet might be proud to call his own.

BRANDER MATTHEWS.

*Columbia University
in the City of New York.*

FIFTY YEARS & OTHER POEMS

FIFTY YEARS & OTHER POEMS

FIFTY YEARS

1863-1913

O brothers mine, to-day we stand
   Where half a century sweeps our ken,
Since God, through Lincoln's ready hand,
   Struck off our bonds and made us men.

Just fifty years — a winter's day —
   As runs the history of a race;
Yet, as we look back o'er the way,
   How distant seems our starting place!

Look farther back! Three centuries!
   To where a naked, shivering score,
Snatched from their haunts across the seas,
   Stood, wild-eyed, on Virginia's shore.

Far, far the way that we have trod,
   From heathen kraals and jungle dens,
To freedmen, freemen, sons of God,
   Americans and Citizens.

A part of His unknown design,
   We've lived within a mighty age;
And we have helped to write a line
   On history's most wondrous page.

[1]

A few black bondmen strewn along
   The borders of our eastern coast,
Now grown a race, ten million strong,
   An upward, onward marching host.

Then let us here erect a stone,
   To mark the place, to mark the time;
A witness to God's mercies shown,
   A pledge to hold this day sublime.

And let that stone an altar be,
   Whereon thanksgivings we may lay,
Where we, in deep humility,
   For faith and strength renewed may pray.

With open hearts ask from above
   New zeal, new courage and new pow'rs,
That we may grow more worthy of
   This country and this land of ours.

For never let the thought arise
   That we are here on sufferance bare;
Outcasts, asylumed 'neath these skies,
   And aliens without part or share.

This land is ours by right of birth,
   This land is ours by right of toil;
We helped to turn its virgin earth,
   Our sweat is in its fruitful soil.

Where once the tangled forest stood, —
    Where flourished once rank weed and thorn, —
Behold the path-traced, peaceful wood,
    The cotton white, the yellow corn.

To gain these fruits that have been earned,
    To hold these fields that have been won,
Our arms have strained, our backs have burned,
    Bent bare beneath a ruthless sun.

That Banner which is now the type
    Of victory on field and flood —
Remember, its first crimson stripe
    Was dyed by Attucks' willing blood.

And never yet has come the cry —
    When that fair flag has been assailed —
For men to do, for men to die,
    That have we faltered or have failed.

We've helped to bear it, rent and torn,
    Through many a hot-breath'd battle breeze;
Held in our hands, it has been borne
    And planted far across the seas.

And never yet—O haughty Land,
    Let us, at least, for this be praised —
Has one black, treason-guided hand
    Ever against that flag been raised.

[3]

Then should we speak but servile words,
　　Or shall we hang our heads in shame?
Stand back of new-come foreign hordes,
　　And fear our heritage to claim?

No! stand erect and without fear,
　　And for our foes let this suffice —
We've bought a rightful sonship here,
　　And we have more than paid the price.

And yet, my brothers, well I know
　　The tethered feet, the pinioned wings,
The spirit bowed beneath the blow,
　　The heart grown faint from wounds and stings;

The staggering force of brutish might,
　　That strikes and leaves us stunned and daezd;
The long, vain waiting through the night
　　To hear some voice for justice raised.

Full well I know the hour when hope
　　Sinks dead, and 'round us everywhere
Hangs stifling darkness, and we grope
　　With hands uplifted in despair.

Courage!　Look out, beyond, and see
　　The far horizon's beckoning span!
Faith in your God-known destiny!
　　We are a part of some great plan.

Because the tongues of Garrison
  And Phillips now are cold in death,
Think you their work can be undone?
  Or quenched the fires lit by their breath?

Think you that John Brown's spirit stops?
  That Lovejoy was but idly slain?
Or do you think those precious drops
  From Lincoln's heart were shed in vain?

That for which millions prayed and sighed,
  That for which tens of thousands fought,
For which so many freely died,
  God cannot let it come to naught.

TO AMERICA

How would you have us, as we are?
Or sinking 'neath the load we bear?
Our eyes fixed forward on a star?
Or gazing empty at despair?

Rising or falling? Men or things?
With dragging pace or footsteps fleet?
Strong, willing sinews in your wings?
Or tightening chains about your feet?

[5]

O BLACK AND UNKNOWN BARDS

O black and unknown bards of long ago,
How came your lips to touch the sacred fire?
How, in your darkness, did you come to know
The power and beauty of the minstrel's lyre?
Who first from midst his bonds lifted his eyes?
Who first from out the still watch, lone and long,
Feeling the ancient faith of prophets rise
Within his dark-kept soul, burst into song?

Heart of what slave poured out such melody
As "Steal away to Jesus"? On its strains
His spirit must have nightly floated free,
Though still about his hands he felt his chains.
Who heard great "Jordan roll"? Whose star-
    ward eye
Saw chariot "swing low"? And who was he
That breathed that comforting, melodic sigh,
"Nobody knows de trouble I see"?

What merely living clod, what captive thing,
Could up toward God through all its darkness
    grope,
And find within its deadened heart to sing
These songs of sorrow, love, and faith, and hope?
How did it catch that subtle undertone,
That note in music heard not with the ears?

How sound the elusive reed so seldom blown,
Which stirs the soul or melts the heart to tears.

Not that great German master in his dream
Of harmonies that thundered amongst the stars
At the creation, ever heard a theme
Nobler than "Go down, Moses." Mark its
    bars,
How like a mighty trumpet-call they stir
The blood. Such are the notes that men have
    sung
Going to valorous deeds; such tones there were
That helped make history when Time was
    young.

There is a wide, wide wonder in it all,
That from degraded rest and servile toil
The fiery spirit of the seer should call
These simple children of the sun and soil.
O black slave singers, gone, forgot, unfamed,
You — you alone, of all the long, long line
Of those who've sung untaught, unknown, un-
    named,
Have stretched out upward, seeking the divine.

You sang not deeds of heroes or of kings;
No chant of bloody war, no exulting pean
Of arms-won triumphs; but your humble strings
You touched in chord with music empyrean.

[7]

You sang far better than you knew; the songs
That for your listeners' hungry hearts sufficed
Still live,—but more than this to you belongs:
You sang a race from wood and stone to Christ.

O SOUTHLAND!

O Southland! O Southland!
  Have you not heard the call,
The trumpet blown, the word made known
  To the nations, one and all?
The watchword, the hope-word,
  Salvation's present plan?
A gospel new, for all—for you:
  Man shall be saved by man.

O Southland! O Southland!
  Do you not hear to-day
The mighty beat of onward feet,
  And know you not their way?
'Tis forward, 'tis upward,
  On to the fair white arch
Of Freedom's dome, and there is room
  For each man who would march.

O Southland, fair Southland!
  Then why do you still cling
To an idle age and a musty page,
  To a dead and useless thing?

'Tis springtime! 'Tis work-time!
  The world is young again!
And God's above, and God is love,
  And men are only men.

O Southland! my Southland!
  O birthland! do not shirk
The toilsome task, nor respite ask,
  But gird you for the work.
Remember, remember
  That weakness stalks in pride;
That he is strong who helps along
  The faint one at his side.

To HORACE BUMSTEAD

Have you been sore discouraged in the fight,
  And even sometimes weighted by the thought
  That those with whom and those for whom
      you fought
Lagged far behind, or dared but faintly smite?
And that the opposing forces in their might
  Of blind inertia rendered as for naught
  All that throughout the long years had been
      wrought,
And powerless each blow for Truth and Right?

If so, take new and greater courage then,
  And think no more withouten help you stand;
  For sure as God on His eternal throne
Sits, mindful of the sinful deeds of men,
  — The awful Sword of Justice in His hand, —
  You shall not, no, you shall not, fight alone.

THE COLOR SERGEANT

(*On an Incident at the Battle of San Juan Hill*)

Under a burning tropic sun,
With comrades around him lying,
A trooper of the sable Tenth
Lay wounded, bleeding, dying.

First in the charge up the fort-crowned hill,
His company's guidon bearing,
He had rushed where the leaden hail fell fast,
Not death nor danger fearing.

He fell in the front where the fight grew fierce,
Still faithful in life's last labor;
Black though his skin, yet his heart as true
As the steel of his blood-stained saber.

And while the battle around him rolled,
Like the roar of a sullen breaker,
He closed his eyes on the bloody scene,
And presented arms to his Maker.

There he lay, without honor or rank,
But, still, in a grim-like beauty;
Despised of men for his humble race,
Yet true, in death, to his duty.

THE BLACK MAMMY

O whitened head entwined in turban gay,
O kind black face, O crude, but tender hand,
O foster-mother in whose arms there lay
The race whose sons are masters of the land!
It was thine arms that sheltered in their fold,
It was thine eyes that followed through the
      length
Of infant days these sons. In times of old
It was thy breast that nourished them to
      strength.

So often hast thou to thy bosom pressed
The golden head, the face and brow of snow;
So often has it 'gainst thy broad, dark breast
Lain, set off like a quickened cameo.
Thou simple soul, as cuddling down that babe
With thy sweet croon, so plaintive and so wild,
Came ne'er the thought to thee, swift like a
      stab,
That it some day might crush thine own black
      child?

FATHER, FATHER ABRAHAM

(*On the Anniversary of Lincoln's Birth*)

Father, Father Abraham,
　To-day look on us from above;
On us, the offspring of thy faith,
　The children of thy Christ-like love.

For that which we have humbly wrought,
　Give us to-day thy kindly smile;
Wherein we've failed or fallen short,
　Bear with us, Father, yet awhile.

Father, Father Abraham,
　To-day we lift our hearts to thee,
Filled with the thought of what great price
　Was paid, that we might ransomed be.

To-day we consecrate ourselves
　Anew in hand and heart and brain,
To send this judgment down the years:
　The ransom was not paid in vain.

BROTHERS

See! There he stands; not brave, but with an
    air
Of sullen stupor. Mark him well! Is he
Not more like brute than man? Look in his eye!
No light is there; none, save the glint that shines
In the now glaring, and now shifting orbs
Of some wild animal caught in the hunter's trap.

How came this beast in human shape and
        form?
Speak, man! — We call you man because you
        wear
His shape — How are you thus? Are you not
        from
That docile, child-like, tender-hearted race
Which we have known three centuries? Not
        from
That more than faithful race which through
        three wars
Fed our dear wives and nursed our helpless
        babes
Without a single breach of trust? Speak out!

I am, and am not.

Then who, why are you?

I am a thing not new, I am as old
As human nature. I am that which lurks,
Ready to spring whenever a bar is loosed;
The ancient trait which fights incessantly
Against restraint, balks at the upward climb;
The weight forever seeking to obey
The law of downward pull;—and I am more:
The bitter fruit am I of planted seed;
The resultant, the inevitable end
Of evil forces and the powers of wrong.

Lessons in degradation, taught and learned,
The memories of cruel sights and deeds,
The pent-up bitterness, the unspent hate
Filtered through fifteen generations have
Sprung up and found in me sporadic life.
In me the muttered curse of dying men,
On me the stain of conquered women, and
Consuming me the fearful fires of lust,
Lit long ago, by other hands than mine.
In me the down-crushed spirit, the hurled-back
      prayers
Of wretches now long dead, — their dire be-
      quests.—
In me the echo of the stifled cry
Of children for their bartered mothers' breasts.
    I claim no race, no race claims me; I am
No more than human dregs; degenerate;
The monstrous offspring of the monster, Sin;

I am — just what I am. . . . The race that fed
Your wives and nursed your babes would do the
      same
To-day, but I —

              Enough, the brute must die!
Quick! Chain him to that oak! It will resist
The fire much longer than this slender pine.
Now bring the fuel! Pile it 'round him! Wait!
Pile not so fast or high! or we shall lose
The agony and terror in his face.
And now the torch! Good fuel that! the flames
Already leap head-high. Ha! hear that shriek!
And there's another! wilder than the first.
Fetch water! Water! Pour a little on
The fire, lest it should burn too fast. Hold so!
Now let it slowly blaze again. See there!
He squirms! He groans! His eyes bulge wildly
      out,
Searching around in vain appeal for help!
Another shriek, the last! Watch how the flesh
Grows crisp and hangs till, turned to ash, it sifts
Down through the coils of chain that hold erect
The ghastly frame against the bark-scorched
      tree.

    Stop! to each man no more than one man's
      share.
You take that bone, and you this tooth; the
      chain —

Let us divide its links; this skull, of course,
In fair division, to the leader comes.

And now his fiendish crime has been
     avenged;
Let us back to our wives and children. — Say,
What did he mean by those last muttered words,
" Brothers in spirit, brothers in deed are we"?

FRAGMENT

The hand of Fate cannot be stayed,
The course of Fate cannot be steered,
By all the gods that man has made,
Nor all the devils he has feared,
Not by the prayers that might be prayed
In all the temples he has reared.

See! In your very midst there dwell
Ten thousand thousand blacks, a wedge
Forged in the furnaces of hell,
And sharpened to a cruel edge
By wrong and by injustice fell,
And driven by hatred as a sledge.

A wedge so slender at the start —
Just twenty slaves in shackles bound —
And yet, which split the land apart

With shrieks of war and battle sound,
Which pierced the nation's very heart,
And still lies cankering in the wound.

Not all the glory of your pride,
Preserved in story and in song,
Can from the judging future hide,
Through all the coming ages long,
That though you bravely fought and died,
You fought and died for what was wrong.

'Tis fixed — for them that violate
The eternal laws, naught shall avail
Till they their error expiate;
Nor shall their unborn children fail
To pay the full required weight
Into God's great, unerring scale.

Think not repentance can redeem,
That sin his wages can withdraw;
No, think as well to change the scheme
Of worlds that move in reverent awe;
Forgiveness is an idle dream,
God is not love, no, God is law.

THE WHITE WITCH

O, brothers mine, take care! Take care!
The great white witch rides out to-night,
Trust not your prowess nor your strength;
Your only safety lies in flight;
For in her glance there is a snare,
And in her smile there is a blight.

The great white witch you have not seen?
Then, younger brothers mine, forsooth,
Like nursery children you have looked
For ancient hag and snaggled tooth;
But no, not so; the witch appears
In all the glowing charms of youth.

Her lips are like carnations red,
Her face like new-born lilies fair,
Her eyes like ocean waters blue,
She moves with subtle grace and air,
And all about her head there floats
The golden glory of her hair.

But though she always thus appears
In form of youth and mood of mirth,
Unnumbered centuries are hers,

The infant planets saw her birth;
The child of throbbing Life is she,
Twin sister to the greedy earth.

And back behind those smiling lips,
And down within those laughing eyes,
And underneath the soft caress
Of hand and voice and purring sighs,
The shadow of the panther lurks,
The spirit of the vampire lies.

For I have seen the great white witch,
And she has led me to her lair,
And I have kissed her red, red lips
And cruel face so white and fair;
Around me she has twined her arms,
And bound me with her yellow hair.

I felt those red lips burn and sear
My body like a living coal;
Obeyed the power of those eyes
As the needle trembles to the pole;
And did not care although I felt
The strength go ebbing from my soul.

Oh! she has seen your strong young limbs,
And heard your laughter loud and gay,
And in your voices she has caught

The echo of a far-off day,
When man was closer to the earth;
And she has marked you for her prey.

She feels the old Antæan strength
In you, the great dynamic beat
Of primal passions, and she sees
In you the last besieged retreat
Of love relentless, lusty, fierce,
Love pain-ecstatic, cruel-sweet.

O, brothers mine, take care! Take care!
The great white witch rides out to-night.
O, younger brothers mine, beware!
Look not upon her beauty bright;
For in her glance there is a snare,
And in her smile there is a blight.

MOTHER NIGHT

Eternities before the first-born day,
    Or ere the first sun fledged his wings of flame,
    Calm Night, the everlasting and the same,
A brooding mother over chaos lay.
And whirling suns shall blaze and then decay,
    Shall run their fiery courses and then claim
    The haven of the darkness whence they came;
Back to Nirvanic peace shall grope their way.

So when my feeble sun of life burns out,
    And sounded is the hour for my long sleep,
    I shall, full weary of the feverish light,
Welcome the darkness without fear or doubt,
    And heavy-lidded, I shall softly creep
    Into the quiet bosom of the Night.

THE YOUNG WARRIOR

Mother, shed no mournful tears,
But gird me on my sword;
And give no utterance to thy fears,
But bless me with thy word.

The lines are drawn! The fight is on!
A cause is to be won!
Mother, look not so white and wan;
Give Godspeed to thy son.

Now let thine eyes my way pursue
Where'er my footsteps fare;
And when they lead beyond thy view,
Send after me a prayer.

But pray not to defend from harm,
Nor danger to dispel;
Pray, rather, that with steadfast arm
I fight the battle well.

Pray, mother of mine, that I always keep
My heart and purpose strong,
My sword unsullied and ready to leap
Unsheathed against the wrong.

THE GLORY OF THE DAY WAS
IN HER FACE

The glory of the day was in her face,
The beauty of the night was in her eyes.
And over all her loveliness, the grace
Of Morning blushing in the early skies.

And in her voice, the calling of the dove;
Like music of a sweet, melodious part.
And in her smile, the breaking light of love;
And all the gentle virtues in her heart.

And now the glorious day, the beauteous night,
The birds that signal to their mates at dawn,
To my dull ears, to my tear-blinded sight
Are one with all the dead, since she is gone.

SONNET

(*From the Spanish of Plácido*)

Enough of love! Let break its every hold!
  Ended my youthful folly! for I know
  That, like the dazzling, glister-shedding snow,
Celia, thou art beautiful, but cold.
I do not find in thee that warmth which glows,
  Which, all these dreary days, my heart has
      sought,
  That warmth without which love is lifeless,
      naught
More than a painted fruit, a waxen rose.

Such love as thine, scarce can it bear love's name,
  Deaf to the pleading notes of his sweet lyre,
A frank, impulsive heart I wish to claim,
  A heart that blindly follows its desire.
I wish to embrace a woman full of flame,
  I want to kiss a woman made of fire.

FROM THE SPANISH

Twenty years go by on noiseless feet,
He returns, and once again they meet,
She exclaims, "Good heavens! and is that he?"
He mutters, "My God! and that is she!"

[25]

FROM THE GERMAN OF UHLAND

Three students once tarried over the Rhine,
And into Frau Wirthin's turned to dine.

"Say, hostess, have you good beer and wine?
And where is that pretty daughter of thine?"

"My beer and wine is fresh and clear.
My daughter lies on her funeral bier."

They softly tipped into the room;
She lay there in the silent gloom.

The first the white cloth gently raised,
And tearfully upon her gazed.

"If thou wert alive, O, lovely maid,
My heart at thy feet would to-day be laid!"

The second covered her face again,
And turned away with grief and pain.

"Ah, thou upon thy snow-white bier!
And I have loved thee so many a year."

The third drew back again the veil,
And kissed the lips so cold and pale.

"I've loved thee always, I love thee to-day,
And will love thee, yes, forever and aye!"

BEFORE A PAINTING

I knew not who had wrought with skill so fine
   What I beheld; nor by what laws of art
   He had created life and love and heart
On canvas, from mere color, curve and line.
Silent I stood and made no move or sign;
   Not with the crowd, but reverently apart;
   Nor felt the power my rooted limbs to start,
But mutely gazed upon that face divine.

And over me the sense of beauty fell,
   As music over a raptured listener to
     The deep-voiced organ breathing out a
      hymn;
Or as on one who kneels, his beads to tell,
   There falls the aureate glory filtered through
     The windows in some old cathedral dim.

I HEAR THE STARS STILL SINGING

   I hear the stars still singing
   To the beautiful, silent night,
   As they speed with noiseless winging
   Their ever westward flight.
   I hear the waves still falling
   On the stretch of lonely shore,
   But the sound of a sweet voice calling
   I shall hear, alas! no more.

GIRL OF FIFTEEN

Girl of fifteen,
I see you each morning from my window
As you pass on your way to school.
I do more than see, I watch you.
I furtively draw the curtain aside.
And my heart leaps through my eyes
And follows you down the street;
Leaving me behind, half-hid
And wholly ashamed.

What holds me back,
Half-hid behind the curtains and wholly
    ashamed,
But my forty years beyond your fifteen?

Girl of fifteen, as you pass
There passes, too, a lightning flash of time
In which you lift those forty summers off my
    head,
And take those forty winters out of my heart.

THE SUICIDE

For fifty years,
Cruel, insatiable Old World,
You have punched me over the heart
Till you made me cough blood.
The few paltry things I gathered
You snatched out of my hands.
You have knocked the cup from my thirsty lips.
You have laughed at my hunger of body and
    soul.

You look at me now and think,
"He is still strong,
There ought to be twenty more years of good
    punching there.
At the end of that time he will be old and broken,
Not able to strike back,
But cringing and crying for leave
To live a little longer."

Those twenty, pitiful, extra years
Would please you more than the fifty past,
Would they not, Old World?
Well, I hold them up before your greedy eyes,
And snatch them away as I laugh in your face,
Ha! Ha!
Bang —!

DOWN BY THE CARIB SEA

I

Sunrise in the Tropics

Sol, Sol, mighty lord of the tropic zone,
Here I wait with the trembling stars
To see thee once more take thy throne.

There the patient palm tree watching
Waits to say, "Good morn" to thee,
And a throb of expectation
Pulses through the earth and me.

Now, o'er nature falls a hush,
Look! the East is all a-blush;
And a growing crimson crest
Dims the late stars in the west;
Now, a flood of golden light
Sweeps across the silver night,
Swift the pale moon fades away
Before the light-girt King of Day,
See! the miracle is done!
Once more behold! The Sun!

II

Los Cigarillos

This is the land of the dark-eyed *gente*,
Of the *dolce far niente*,
Where we dream away
Both the night and day,
At night-time in sleep our dreams we invoke,
Our dreams come by day through the redolent
    smoke,
As it lazily curls,
And slowly unfurls
From our lips,
And the tips
Of our fragrant *cigarillos*.
For life in the tropics is only a joke,
So we pass it in dreams, and we pass it in smoke,
Smoke — smoke — smoke.

Tropical constitutions
Call for occasional revolutions;
But after that's through,
Why there's nothing to do
But smoke — smoke;

For life in the tropics is only a joke,
So we pass it in dreams, and we pass it in smoke,
Smoke — smoke — smoke.

[31]

III

Teestay

Of tropic sensations, the worst
Is, *sin duda*, the tropical thirst.

When it starts in your throat and constantly
    grows,
Till you feel that it reaches down to your toes,
When your mouth tastes like fur
And your tongue turns to dust,
There's but one thing to do,
And do it you must,
Drink *teestay*.

Teestay, a drink with a history,
A delicious, delectable mystery,
"*Cinco centavos el vaso, señor*,"
If you take one, you will surely want more.

Teestay, *teestay*,
The national drink on a feast day;
How it coolingly tickles,
As downward it trickles,
Teestay, *teestay*.

And you wish, as you take it down at a quaff,
That your neck was constructed à la giraffe.
Teestay, *teestay*.

IV

The Lottery Girl

"Lottery, lottery,
  Take a chance at the lottery?
Take a ticket,
Or, better, take two;
Who knows what the future
May hold for you?
Lottery, lottery,
Take a chance at the lottery?"

Oh, limpid-eyed girl,
I would take every chance,
If only the prize
Were a love-flashing glance
From your fathomless eyes.

"Lottery, lottery,
  Try your luck at the lottery?
Consider the size
Of the capital prize,
And take tickets
For the lottery.
Tickets, *señor?* Tickets, *señor?*
Take a chance at the lottery?"

Oh, crimson-lipped girl,
With the magical smile,

[33]

I would count that the gamble
Were well worth the while,
Not a chance would I miss,
If only the prize
Were a honey-bee kiss
Gathered in sips
From those full-ripened lips,
And a love-flashing glance
From your eyes.

V

The Dancing Girl

Do you know what it is to dance?
Perhaps, you do know, in a fashion;
But by dancing I mean,
Not what's generally seen,
But dancing of fire and passion,
Of fire and delirious passion.

With a dusky-haired *señorita*,
Her dark, misty eyes near your own,
And her scarlet-red mouth,
Like a rose of the south,
The reddest that ever was grown,
So close that you catch
Her quick-panting breath
As across your own face it is blown,
With a sigh, and a moan.

[34]

Ah! that is dancing,
As here by the Carib it's known.

Now, whirling and twirling
Like furies we go;
Now, soft and caressing
And sinuously slow;
With an undulating motion,
Like waves on a breeze-kissed ocean:—
And the scarlet-red mouth
Is nearer your own,
And the dark, misty eyes
Still softer have grown.

Ah! that is dancing, that is loving,
As here by the Carib they're known.

VI

Sunset in the Tropics

A silver flash from the sinking sun,
Then a shot of crimson across the sky
That, bursting, lets a thousand colors fly
And riot among the clouds; they run,
Deepening in purple, flaming in gold,
Changing, and opening fold after fold,
Then fading through all of the tints of the rose
    into gray,
Till, taking quick fright at the coming night,
They rush out down the west,
In hurried quest
Of the fleeing day.

Now above where the tardiest color flares
    a moment yet,
One point of light, now two, now three are set
To form the starry stairs, —
And, in her fire-fly crown,
Queen Night, on velvet slippered feet, comes
    softly down.

AND THE GREATEST OF THESE IS WAR

Around the council-board of Hell, with Satan at
    their head,
The Three Great Scourges of humanity sat.
Gaunt Famine, with hollow cheek and voice,
    arose and spoke,—
"O, Prince, I have stalked the earth,
And my victims by ten thousands I have slain,
I have smitten old and young.
Mouths of the helpless old moaning for bread,
    I have filled with dust;
And I have laughed to see a crying babe tug at
    the shriveling breast
Of its mother, dead and cold.
I have heard the cries and prayers of men go up
    to a tearless sky,
And fall back upon an earth of ashes;
But, heedless, I have gone on with my work.
'Tis thus, O, Prince, that I have scourged man-
    kind."

And Satan nodded his head.

Pale Pestilence, with stenchful breath, then
    spoke and said,—
"Great Prince, my brother, Famine, attacks
    the poor.

He is most terrible against the helpless and the
    old.
But I have made a charnel-house of the mightiest
    cities of men.
When I strike, neither their stores of gold or of
    grain avail.
With a breath I lay low their strongest, and
    wither up their fairest.
I come upon them without warning, lancing
    invisible death.
From me they flee with eyes and mouths dis-
    tended;
I poison the air for which they gasp, and I strike
    them down fleeing.
'Tis thus, great Prince, that I have scourged
    mankind.''

And Satan nodded his head.

Then the red monster, War, rose up and spoke,—
His blood-shot eyes glared 'round him, and his
    thundering voice
Echoed through the murky vaults of Hell. —
" O, mighty Prince, my brothers, Famine and
    Pestilence,
Have slain their thousands and ten thousands,—
    true;
But the greater their victories have been,
The more have they wakened in Man's breast

The God-like attributes of sympathy, of brother-
    hood and love
And made of him a searcher after wisdom.
But I arouse in Man the demon and the brute,
I plant black hatred in his heart and red re-
    venge.
From the summit of fifty thousand years of
    upward climb
I haul him down to the level of the start, back
    to the wolf.
I give him claws.
I set his teeth into his brother's throat.
I make him drunk with his brother's blood.
And I laugh ho! ho! while he destroys himself.
O, mighty Prince, not only do I slay,
But I draw Man hellward."

And Satan smiled, stretched out his hand, and
    said, —
" O War, of all the scourges of humanity, I
    crown you chief."

And Hell rang with the acclamation of the
    Fiends.

A MID-DAY DREAMER

I love to sit alone, and dream,
And dream, and dream;
In fancy's boat to softly glide
Along some stream
Where fairy palaces of gold
And crystal bright
Stand all along the glistening shore:
A wondrous sight.

My craft is built of ivory,
With silver oars,
The sails are spun of golden threads,
And priceless stores
Of precious gems adorn its prow,
And 'round its mast
An hundred silken cords are set
To hold it fast.

My galley-slaves are sprightly elves
Who, as they row,
And as their shining oars they swing
Them to and fro,
Keep time to music wafted on
The scented air,
Made by the mermaids as they comb
Their golden hair.

And I the while lie idly back,
And dream, and dream,
And let them row me where they will
Adown the stream.

THE TEMPTRESS

Old Devil, when you come with horns and tail,
With diabolic grin and crafty leer;
I say, such bogey-man devices wholly fail
To waken in my heart a single fear.

But when you wear a form I know so well,
A form so human, yet so near divine;
'Tis then I fall beneath the magic of your spell,
'Tis then I know the vantage is not mine.

Ah! when you take your horns from off your
            head,
And soft and fragrant hair is in their place;
I must admit I fear the tangled path I tread
When that dear head is laid against my face.

And at what time you change your baleful eyes
For stars that melt into the gloom of night,
All of my courage, my dear fellow, quickly flies;
I know my chance is slim to win the fight.

And when, instead of charging down to wreck
Me on a red-hot pitchfork in your hand,
You throw a pair of slender arms about my neck,
I dare not trust the ground on which I stand.

Whene'er in place of using patent wile,
Or trying to frighten me with horrid grin,
You tempt me with two crimson lips curved in a
    smile;
Old Devil, I must really own, you win.

GHOSTS OF THE OLD YEAR

The snow has ceased its fluttering flight,
The wind sunk to a whisper light,
An ominous stillness fills the night,
    A pause — a hush.
At last, a sound that breaks the spell,
Loud, clanging mouthings of a bell,
That through the silence peal and swell,
    And roll, and rush.

What does this brazen tongue declare,
That falling on the midnight air
Brings to my heart a sense of care
    Akin to fright?
'Tis telling that the year is dead,
The New Year come, the Old Year fled,
Another leaf before me spread
    On which to write.

[42]

It tells the deeds that were not done,
It tells of races never run,
Of victories that were not won,
   Barriers unleaped.
It tells of many a squandered day,
Of slighted gems and treasured clay,
Of precious stores not laid away,
   Of fields unreaped.

And so the years go swiftly by,
Each, coming, brings ambitions high,
And each, departing, leaves a sigh
   Linked to the past.
Large resolutions, little deeds;
Thus, filled with aims unreached, life speeds
Until the blotted record reads,
   "Failure!" at last.

THE GHOST OF DEACON BROWN

In a backwoods town
Lived Deacon Brown,
And he was a miser old;
He would trust no bank,
So he dug, and sank
In the ground a box of gold,
Down deep in the ground a box of gold.

[43]

He hid his gold,
As has been told,
He remembered that he did it;
But sad to say,
On the very next day,
He forgot just where he hid it:
To find his gold he tried and tried
Till he grew faint and sick, and died.

Then on each dark and gloomy night
A form in phosphorescent white,
A genuine hair-raising sight,
Would wander through the town.
And as it slowly roamed around,
With a spade it dug each foot of ground;
So the folks about
Said there was no doubt
'Twas the ghost of Deacon Brown.

Around the church
This Ghost would search,
And whenever it would see
The passers-by
Take wings and fly
It would laugh in ghostly glee,
Hee, hee!—it would laugh in ghostly glee.

And so the town
Went quickly down,

For they said that it was haunted;
And doors and gates,
So the story states,
Bore a notice, "Tenants wanted."

And the town is now for let,
But the ghost is digging yet.

"LAZY"

Some men enjoy the constant strife
Of days with work and worry rife,
But that is not my dream of life:
    I think such men are crazy.
For me, a life with worries few,
A job of nothing much to do,
Just pelf enough to see me through:
    I fear that I am lazy.

On winter mornings cold and drear,
When six o'clock alarms I hear,
'Tis then I love to shift my ear,
    And hug my downy pillows.
When in the shade it's ninety-three,
No job in town looks good to me,
I'd rather loaf down by the sea,
    And watch the foaming billows.

Some people think the world's a school,
Where labor is the only rule;
But I'll not make myself a mule,
    And don't you ever doubt it.
I know that work may have its use,
But still I feel that's no excuse
For turning it into abuse;
    What do *you* think about it?

Let others fume and sweat and boil,
And scratch and dig for golden spoil,
And live the life of work and toil,
    Their lives to labor giving.
But what is gold when life is sped,
And life is short, as has been said,
And we are such a long time dead,
    I'll spend my life in living.

OMAR

Old Omar, jolly sceptic, it may be
That, after all, you found the magic key
To life and all its mystery, and I
Must own you have almost persuaded me.

DEEP IN THE QUIET WOOD

Are you bowed down in heart?
Do you but hear the clashing discords and the
    din of life?
Then come away, come to the peaceful wood,
Here bathe your soul in silence. Listen! Now,
From out the palpitating solitude
Do you not catch, yet faint, elusive strains?
They are above, around, within you, every-
    where.
Silently listen! Clear, and still more clear,
    they come.
They bubble up in rippling notes, and swell in
    singing tones.
Not let your soul run the whole gamut of the
    wondrous scale
Until, responsive to the tonic chord,
It touches the diapason of God's grand cathe-
    dral organ,
Filling earth for you with heavenly peace
And holy harmonies.

VOLUPTAS

To chase a never-reached mirage
Across the hot, white sand,
And choke and die, while gazing on
Its green and watered strand.

[47]

THE WORD OF AN ENGINEER

" She's built of steel
  From deck to keel,
  And bolted strong and tight;
  In scorn she'll sail
  The fiercest gale,
  And pierce the darkest night.

" The builder's art
  Has proved each part
  Throughout her breadth and length;
  Deep in the hulk,
  Of her mighty bulk,
  Ten thousand Titans' strength."

The tempest howls,
The Ice Wolf prowls,
The winds they shift and veer,
But calm I sleep,
And faith I keep
In the word of an engineer.

Along the trail
Of the slender rail
The train, like a nightmare, flies
And dashes on
Through the black-mouthed yawn
Where the cavernous tunnel lies.

Over the ridge,
Across the bridge,
Swung twixt the sky and hell,
On an iron thread
Spun from the head
Of the man in a draughtsman's cell.

And so we ride
Over land and tide,
Without a thought of fear —
Man never had
The faith in God
That he has in an engineer!

LIFE

Out of the infinite sea of eternity
To climb, and for an instant stand
Upon an island speck of time.

From the impassible peace of the darkness
To wake, and blink at the garish light
Through one short hour of fretfulness.

SLEEP

O Sleep, thou kindest minister to man,
    Silent distiller of the balm of rest,
How wonderful thy power, when naught else can,
    To soothe the torn and sorrow-laden breast!
When bleeding hearts no comforter can find,
    When burdened souls droop under weight of
        woe,
When thought is torture to the troubled mind,
    When grief-relieving tears refuse to flow;
'Tis then thou comest on soft-beating wings,
    And sweet oblivion's peace from them is shed;
But ah, the old pain that the waking brings!
    That lives again so soon as thou art fled!

Man, why should thought of death cause thee
      to weep;
Since death be but an endless, dreamless sleep?

PRAYER AT SUNRISE

O mighty, powerful, dark-dispelling sun,
Now thou art risen, and thy day begun.
How shrink the shrouding mists before thy face,
As up thou spring'st to thy diurnal race!
How darkness chases darkness to the west,
As shades of light on light rise radiant from thy
    crest!
For thee, great source of strength, emblem of
    might,
In hours of darkest gloom there is no night.
Thou shinest on though clouds hide thee from
    sight,
And through each break thou sendest down thy
    light.

O greater Maker of this Thy great sun,
Give me the strength this one day's race to run,
Fill me with light, fill me with sun-like strength,
Fill me with joy to rob the day its length.
Light from within, light that will outward shine,
Strength to make strong some weaker heart
    than mine,
Joy to make glad each soul that feels its touch;
Great Father of the sun, I ask this much.

[51]

THE GIFT TO SING

Sometimes the mist overhangs my path,
And blackening clouds about me cling;
But, oh, I have a magic way
To turn the gloom to cheerful day —
   I softly sing.

And if the way grows darker still,
Shadowed by Sorrow's somber wing,
With glad defiance in my throat,
I pierce the darkness with a note,
   And sing, and sing.

I brood not over the broken past,
Nor dread whatever time may bring;
No nights are dark, no days are long,
While in my heart there swells a song,
   And I can sing.

MORNING, NOON AND NIGHT

When morning shows her first faint flush,
I think of the tender blush
That crept so gently to your cheek
When first my love I dared to speak;
How, in your glance, a dawning ray
Gave promise of love's perfect day.

When, in the ardent breath of noon,
The roses with passion swoon;
There steals upon me from the air
The scent that lurked within your hair;
I touch your hand, I clasp your form—
Again your lips are close and warm.

When comes the night with beauteous skies,
I think of your tear-dimmed eyes,
Their mute entreaty that I stay,
Although your lips sent me away;
And then falls memory's bitter blight,
And dark — so dark becomes the night.

HER EYES TWIN POOLS

Her eyes, twin pools of mystic light,
The blend of star-sheen and black night;
O'er which, to sound their glamouring haze,
A man might bend, and vainly gaze.

Her eyes, twin pools so dark and deep,
In which life's ancient mysteries sleep;
Wherein, to seek the quested goal,
A man might plunge, and lose his soul.

THE AWAKENING

I dreamed that I was a rose
That grew beside a lonely way,
Close by a path none ever chose,
And there I lingered day by day.
Beneath the sunshine and the show'r
I grew and waited there apart,
Gathering perfume hour by hour,
And storing it within my heart,
   Yet, never knew,
Just why I waited there and grew.

I dreamed that you were a bee
That one day gaily flew along,
You came across the hedge to me,
And sang a soft, love-burdened song.
You brushed my petals with a kiss,
I woke to gladness with a start,
And yielded up to you in bliss
The treasured fragrance of my heart;
   And then I knew
That I had waited there for you.

BEAUTY THAT IS NEVER OLD

When buffeted and beaten by life's storms,
When by the bitter cares of life oppressed,
I want no surer haven than your arms,
I want no sweeter heaven than your breast.

When over my life's way there falls the blight
Of sunless days, and nights of starless skies;
Enough for me, the calm and steadfast light
That softly shines within your loving eyes.

The world, for me, and all the world can hold
Is circled by your arms; for me there lies,
Within the lights and shadows of your eyes,
The only beauty that is never old.

VENUS IN A GARDEN

'Twas at early morning,
The dawn was blushing in her purple bed,
When in a sweet, embowered garden
She, the fairest of the goddesses,
The lovely Venus,
Roamed amongst the roses white and red.
She sought for flowers
To make a garland
For her golden head.

Snow-white roses, blood-red roses,
In that sweet garden close,
Offered incense to the goddess:
Both the white and the crimson rose.

White roses, red roses, blossoming:
But the fair Venus knew
The crimson roses had gained their hue
From the hearts that for love had bled;
And the goddess made a garland
Gathered from the roses red.

VASHTI

I sometimes take you in my dreams to a far-
off land I used to know,
Back in the ages long ago; a land of palms and
languid streams.

A land, by night, of jeweled skies, by day, of
shores that glistened bright,
Within whose arms, outstretched and white, a
sapphire sea lay crescent-wise.

Where twilight fell like silver floss, where rose
the golden moon half-hid
Behind a shadowy pyramid; a land beneath the
Southern Cross.

And there the days dreamed in their flight, each
one a poem chanted through,
Which at its close was merged into the muted
music of the night.

And you were a princess in those days. And I —
I was your serving lad.
But who ever served with heart so glad, or lived
so for a word of praise?

And if that word you chanced to speak, how all
my senses swayed and reeled,
Till low beside your feet I kneeled, with happi-
ness o'erwrought and weak.

If, when your golden cup I bore, you deigned to
lower your eyes to mine,
Eyes cold, yet fervid, like the wine, I knew not
how to wish for more.

I trembled at the thought to dare to gaze upon,
to scrutinize
The deep-sea mystery of your eyes, the sun-lit
splendor of your hair.

To let my timid glances rest upon you long
enough to note
How fair and slender was your throat, how
white the promise of your breast.

But though I did not dare to chance a lingering
look, an open gaze
Upon your beauty's blinding rays, I ventured
many a stolen glance.

I fancy, too, (but could not state what trick of
mind the fancy caused)
At times your eyes upon me paused, and marked
my figure lithe and straight.

Once when my eyes met yours it seemed that in
    your cheek, despite your pride,
A flush arose and swiftly died; or was it some-
    thing that I dreamed?

Within your radiance like the star of morning,
    there I stood and served,
Close by, unheeded, unobserved. You were so
    near, and, yet, so far.

Ah! just to stretch my hand and touch the musky
    sandals on your feet!—
My breaking heart! of rapture sweet it never
    could have held so much.

Oh, beauty-haunted memory! Your face so
    proud, your eyes so calm,
Your body like a slim young palm, and sinuous
    as a willow tree.

Caught up beneath your slender arms, and
    girdled 'round your supple waist,
A robe of curious silk that graced, but only scarce
    concealed your charms.

A golden band about your head, a crimson jewel
    at your throat
Which, when the sunlight on it smote, turned
    to a living heart and bled.

But, oh, that mystic bleeding stone, that work
    of Nature's magic art,
Which mimicked so a wounded heart, could
    never bleed as did my own!

Now after ages long and sad, in this stern land
    we meet anew;
No more a princess proud are you, and I — I am
    no serving lad.

And yet, dividing us, I meet a wider gulf than
    that which stood
Between a princess of the blood and him who
    served low at her feet.

THE REWARD

No greater earthly boon than this I crave,
That those who some day gather 'round my
    grave,
In place of tears, may whisper of me then,
"He sang a song that reached the hearts of
    men."

JINGLES & CROONS

JINGLES & CROONS

SENCE YOU WENT AWAY

Seems lak to me de stars don't shine so bright,
Seems lak to me de sun done loss his light,
Seems lak to me der's nothin' goin' right,
    Sence you went away.

Seems lak to me de sky ain't half so blue,
Seems lak to me dat ev'ything wants you,
Seems lak to me I don't know what to do,
    Sence you went away.

Seems lak to me dat ev'ything is wrong,
Seems lak to me de day's jes twice as long,
Seems lak to me de bird's forgot his song,
    Sence you went away.

Seems lak to me I jes can't he'p but sigh,
Seems lak to me ma th'oat keeps gittin' dry,
Seems lak to me a tear stays in ma eye,
    Sence you went away.

MA LADY'S LIPS AM LIKE DE HONEY
(*Negro Love Song*)

Breeze a-sighin' and a-blowin',
Southern summer night.
Stars a-gleamin' and a-glowin',
Moon jes shinin' right.
Strollin', like all lovers do,
Down de lane wid Lindy Lou;
Honey on her lips to waste;
'Speck I'm gwine to steal a taste.

   Oh, ma lady's lips am like de honey,
   Ma lady's lips am like de rose;
   An' I'm jes like de little bee a-buzzin'
   'Round de flower wha' de nectah grows.
   Ma lady's lips dey smile so temptin',
   Ma lady's teeth so white dey shine,
   Oh, ma lady's lips so tantalizin',
   Ma lady's lips so close to mine.

Bird a-whistlin' and a-swayin'
In de live-oak tree;
Seems to me he keeps a-sayin',
"Kiss dat gal fo' me."
Look heah, Mister Mockin' Bird,
Gwine to take you at yo' word;
If I meets ma Waterloo,
Gwine to blame it all on you.

Oh, ma lady's lips am like de honey,
Ma lady's lips am like de rose;
An' I'm jes like de little bee a-buzzin'
'Round de flower wha' de nectah grows.
Ma lady's lips dey smile so temptin',
Ma lady's teeth so white dey shine,
Oh, ma lady's lips so tantalizin',
Ma lady's lips so close to mine.

Honey in de rose, I spose, is
Put der fo' de bee;
Honey on her lips, I knows, is
Put der jes fo' me.
Seen a sparkle in her eye,
Heard her heave a little sigh;
Felt her kinder squeeze ma han',
'Nuff to make me understan'.

TUNK

(*A Lecture on Modern Education*)

Look heah, Tunk! — Now, ain't dis awful!
    T'ought I sont you off to school.
Don't you know dat you is growin' up to be a
    reg'lah fool?

Whah's dem books dat I's done bought you?
    Look heah, boy, you tell me quick,
Whah's dat Webster blue-back spellah an' dat
    bran' new 'rifmatic?

W'ile I'm t'inkin' you is lahnin' in de school,
    why bless ma soul!
You off in de woods a-playin'. Can't you do like
    you is tole?

Boy, I tell you, it's jes scan'lous d'way dat you
    is goin' on.
An' you sholy go'n be sorry, jes as true as you
    is bo'n.

Heah I'm tryin' hard to raise you as a credit to
    dis race,
An' you tryin' heap much harder fu' to come up
    in disgrace.

Dese de days w'en men don't git up to de top
  by hooks an' crooks;
Tell you now, dey's got to git der standin' on
  a pile o' books.

W'en you sees a darkey goin' to de fiel' as soon
  as light,
Followin' a mule across it f'om de mawnin' tel
  de night,

Wukin' all his life fu' vittles, hoein' 'tween de
  cott'n rows,
W'en he knocks off ole an' tiah'd, ownin' nut'n
  but his clo'es,

You kin put it down to ignunce, aftah all what's
  done an' said,
You kin bet dat dat same darkey ain't got nut'n
  in his head.

Ain't you seed dem w'ite men set'n in der
  awfice? Don't you know
Dey goes der 'bout nine each mawnin'? Bless
  yo' soul, dey's out by fo'.

Dey jes does a little writin'; does dat by some
  easy means;
Gals jes set an' play piannah on dem printin'
  press muchines.

Chile, dem men knows how to figgah, how to
use dat little pen,
An' dey knows dat blue-back spellah f'om be-
ginnin' to de en'.

Dat's de 'fect of education; dat's de t'ing what's
gwine to rule;
Git dem books, you lazy rascal! Git back to yo'
place in school!

NOBODY'S LOOKIN' BUT DE OWL
AND DE MOON

(*A Negro Serenade*)

De river is a-glistenin' in de moonlight,
De owl is set'n high up in de tree;
De little stars am twinklin' wid a sof' light,
De night seems only jes fu' you an' me.
Thoo de trees de breezes am a-sighin',
Breathin' out a sort o' lover's croon,
Der's nobody lookin' or a-spyin',
Nobody but de owl an' de moon.

Nobody's lookin' but de owl an' de moon,
An' de night is balmy; fu' de month is June;
Come den, Honey, won't you? Come to meet
        me soon,
W'ile nobody's lookin' but de owl an' de moon.

I feel so kinder lonely all de daytime,
It seems I raly don't know what to do;
I jes keep sort a-longin' fu' de night-time,
'Cause den I know dat I can be wid you.
An' de thought jes sets my brain a-swayin',
An' my heart a-beatin' to a tune;
Come, de owl won't tell w'at we's a-sayin',
An' cose you know we kin trus' de moon.

[69]

YOU'S SWEET TO YO' MAMMY
JES DE SAME

(*Lullaby*)

Shet yo' eyes, ma little pickaninny, go to sleep
Mammy's watchin' by you all de w'ile;
Daddy is a-wukin' down in de cott'n fiel',
Wukin' fu' his little honey child.
An' yo' mammy's heart is jes a-brimmin' full
     o' lub
Fu' you f'om yo' head down to yo' feet;
Oh, no mattah w'at some othah folks may
     t'ink o' you,
To yo' mammy's heart you's mighty sweet.

You's sweet to yo' mammy jes de same;
Dat's why she calls you Honey fu' yo' name.
Yo' face is black, dat's true,
An' yo' hair is woolly, too,
But, you's sweet to yo' mammy jes de same.

Up der in de big house w'ere dey lib so rich an'
     gran'
Dey's got chillen dat dey lubs, I s'pose;
Chillen dat is purty, oh, but dey can't lub dem
     mo'
Dan yo' mammy lubs you, heaben knows!

Dey may t'ink you's homely, an' yo' clo'es dey
      may be po',
But yo' shinin' eyes, dey hol's a light
Dat, my Honey, w'en you opens dem so big an'
      roun',
Makes you lubly in yo' mammy's sight.

A PLANTATION BACCHANAL

W'en ole Mister Sun gits tiah'd a-hangin'
High up in de sky;
W'en der ain't no thunder and light'nin'
      a-bangin',
An' de crap's done all laid by;
W'en yo' bones ain't achin' wid de rheumatics,
Den yo' ride de mule to town,
Git a great big jug o' de ole corn juice,
An' w'en you drink her down —

       Jes lay away ole Trouble,
       An' dry up all yo' tears;
       Yo' pleasure sho' to double
       An' you bound to lose yo' keers.
       Jes lay away ole Sorrer
       High upon de shelf;
       And never mind to-morrer,
       'Twill take care of itself.

W'en ole Mister Age begins a-stealin'
Thoo yo' back an' knees,
W'en yo' bones an' jints lose der limber feelin',
An' am stiff'nin' by degrees;
Now der's jes one way to feel young and spry,
W'en you heah dem banjos soun'
Git a great big swig o' de ole corn juice,
An' w'en you drink her down —

> Jes lay away ole Trouble,
> An' dry up all yo' tears;
> Yo' pleasure sho' to double
> An' you bound to lose yo' keers.
> Jes lay away ole Sorrer
> High upon de shelf;
> And never mind to-morrer,
> 'Twill take care of itself.

JULY IN GEORGY

I'm back down in ole Georgy w'ere de sun is
     shinin' hot,
W'ere de cawn it is a-tasslin', gittin' ready fu'
     de pot;

W'ere de cott'n is a-openin' an' a-w'itenin' in
     de sun,
An' de ripenin' o' de sugah-cane is mighty nigh
     begun.

An' de locus' is a-singin' f'om eveh bush an'
     tree,
An' you kin heah de hummin' o' de noisy bum-
     blebee;

An' de mule he stan's a-dreamin' an' a-dreamin'
     in de lot,
An' de sun it is a-shinin' mighty hot, hot, hot.

But evehbody is a-restin', fu' de craps is all laid
     by,
An' time fu' de camp-meetin' is a-drawin' purty
     nigh;

An' we's put away de ploughshare, an' we's done
     hung up de spade,
An' we's eatin' watermelon, an' a-layin' in de
     shade.

A BANJO SONG

W'en de banjos wuz a-ringin',
An' de darkies wuz a-singin',
Oh, wuzen dem de good times sho!
All de ole folks would be chattin',
An' de pickaninnies pattin',
As dey heah'd de feet a-shufflin' 'cross de flo'.

An' how we'd dance, an' how we'd sing!
Dance tel de day done break.
An' how dem banjos dey would ring,
An' de cabin flo' would shake!

Come along, come along,
Come along, come along,
Don't you heah dem banjos a-ringin'?

Gib a song, gib a song,
Gib a song, gib a song,
Git yo' feet fixed up fu' a-wingin'.

W'ile de banjos dey go plunka, plunka, plunk,
We'll dance tel de ole flo' shake;
W'ile de feet keep a-goin' chooka, chooka,
      chook,
We'll dance tel de day done break.

[74]

ANSWER TO PRAYER

Der ain't no use in sayin' de Lawd won't answer
 prah;
If you knows how to ax Him, I knows He's
 bound to heah.

De trouble is, some people don't ax de proper
 way,
Den w'en dey git's no answer dey doubts de use
 to pray.

You got to use egzac'ly de 'spressions an' de
 words
To show dat 'tween yo' faith an' works, you
 'pends on works two-thirds.

Now, one time I remember — jes how long
 I won't say —
I thought I'd like a turkey to eat on Chris'mus
 day.

Fu' weeks I dreamed 'bout turkeys, a-struttin'
 in der pride;
But seed no way to get one — widout de Lawd
 pervide.

An' so I went to prayin', I pray'd wid all my
 might;

[75]

"Lawd, sen' *to* me a turkey." I pray'd bofe day an' night.

"Lawd, sen' *to* me a turkey, a big one if you please."
I 'clar to heaben I pray'd so much I mos' wore out ma knees.

I pray'd dat prah so often, I pray'd dat prah so long,
Yet didn't git no turkey, I know'd 'twas sump'n wrong.

So on de night 'fore Chris'mus w'en I got down to pray,
"Lawd, sen' *me* to a turkey," I had de sense to say.

"Lawd, sen' *me* to a turkey." I know dat prah was right,
An' it was sholy answer'd; I got de bird dat night.

DAT GÁL O' MINE

Skin as black an' jes as sof' as a velvet dress,
Teeth as white as ivory — well dey is I guess.

Eyes dat's jes as big an' bright as de evenin'
      star;
An' dat hol' some sort o' light lublier by far.

Hair don't hang 'way down her back; plaited
      up in rows;
Wid de two en's dat's behin' tied wid ribben
      bows.

Han's dat raly wuz'n made fu' hard work, I'm
      sho';
Got a little bit o' foot; weahs a numbah fo'.

You jes oughtah see dat gal Sunday's w'en she
      goes
To de Baptis' meetin' house, dressed in her
      bes' clo'es.

W'en she puts her w'ite dress on an' othah
      things so fine;
Now, Su', don't you know I'm proud o' dat gal
      o' mine.

THE SEASONS

W'en de leaves begin to fall,
An' de fros' is on de ground,
An' de 'simmons is a-ripenin' on de tree;
W'en I heah de dinner call,
An' de chillen gadder 'round,
'Tis den de 'possum is de meat fu' me.

W'en de wintertime am pas'
An' de spring is come at las',
W'en de good ole summer sun begins to shine;
Oh! my thoughts den tek a turn,
An' my heart begins to yearn
Fo' dat watermelon growin' on de vine.

Now, de yeah will sholy bring
'Round a season fu' us all,
Ev'y one kin pick his season f'om de res';
But de melon in de spring,
An' de 'possum in de fall,
Mek it hard to tell which time o' year am bes'.

'POSSUM SONG

(*A Warning*)

'Simmons ripenin' in de fall,
You better run,
Brudder 'Possum, run!
Mockin' bird commence to call,
You better run, Brudder 'Possum, git out de
    way!
You better run, Brudder 'Possum, git out de
    way!
Run some whar an' hide!
Ole moon am sinkin'
Down behin' de tree.
Ole Eph am thinkin'
An' chuckelin' wid glee.
Ole Tige am blinkin'
An' frisky as kin be,
Yo' chances, Brudder 'Possum,
Look mighty slim to me.

Run, run, run, I tell you,
Run, Brudder 'Possum, run!
Run, run, run, I tell you,
Ole Eph's got a gun.
Pickaninnies grinnin'
Waitin' fu' to see de fun.

You better run, Brudder 'Possum, git out de
      way!
Run, Brudder 'Possum, run!

Brudder 'Possum take a tip;
You better run,
Brudder 'Possum, run!
'Tain't no use in actin' flip,
You better run, Brudder 'Possum, git out de
      way!
You better run, Brudder 'Possum, git out de
      way!
Run some whar an' hide.
Dey's gwine to houn' you
All along de line,
W'en dey done foun' you,
Den what's de use in sighin'?
Wid taters roun' you.
You sholy would tase fine—
So listen, Brudder 'Possum,
You better be a-flyin'.

Run, run, run, I tell you,
Run, Brudder 'Possum, run!
Run, run, run, I tell you,
Ole Eph's got a gun.
Pickaninnies grinnin'
Waitin' fu' to see de fun.
You better run, Brudder 'Possum, git out de way!
Run, Brudder 'Possum, run!

BRER RABBIT, YOU'S DE CUTES'
OF 'EM ALL

Once der was a meetin' in de wilderness,
All de critters of creation dey was dar;
Brer Rabbit, Brer 'Possum, Brer Wolf, Brer
    Fox,
King Lion, Mister Terrapin, Mister B'ar.
De question fu' discussion was, "Who is de
    bigges' man?"
Dey 'pinted ole Jedge Owl to decide;
He polished up his spectacles an' put 'em on his
    nose,
An' to the question slowly he replied:

"Brer Wolf am mighty cunnin',
Brer Fox am mighty sly,
Brer Terrapin an' 'Possum — kinder small;
Brer Lion's mighty vicious,
Brer B'ar he's sorter 'spicious,
Brer Rabbit, you's de cutes' of 'em all."

Dis caused a great confusion 'mongst de animals,
Ev'y critter claimed dat he had won de prize;
Dey 'sputed an' dey arg'ed, dey growled an' dey
    roared,
Den putty soon de dus' begin to rise.

Brer Rabbit he jes' stood aside an' urged 'em
      on to fight.
Brer Lion he mos' tore Brer B'ar in two;
W'en dey was all so tiahd dat dey couldn't catch
      der bref
Brer Rabbit he jes' grabbed de prize an' flew.

Brer Wolf am mighty cunnin',
Brer Fox am mighty sly,
Brer Terrapin an' Possum — kinder small;
Brer Lion's mighty vicious,
Brer B'ar he's sorter 'spicious,
Brer Rabbit, you's de cutes' of 'em all.

AN EXPLANATION

Look heah! 'Splain to me de reason
Why you said to Squire Lee,
Der wuz twelve ole chicken thieves
In dis heah town, includin' me.
Ef he tole you dat, my brudder,
He said sump'n dat warn't true;
W'at I said wuz dis, dat der wuz
Twelve, *widout* includin' you.

Oh! .   .   ! —

DE LITTLE PICKANINNY'S GONE
TO SLEEP

Cuddle down, ma honey, in yo' bed,
Go to sleep an' res' yo' little head,
Been a-kind o' ailin' all de day?
Didn't have no sperit fu' to play?
Never min'; to-morrer, w'en you wek,
Daddy's gwine to ride you on his bek,
'Roun' an' roun' de cabin flo' so fas' —
Der! He's closed his little eyes at las'.

De little pickaninny's gone to sleep,
Cuddled in his trundle bed so tiny,
De little pickaninny's gone to sleep,
Closed his little eyes so bright an' shiny.
Hush! an' w'en you walk across de flo'
Step across it very sof' an' slow.
De shadders all aroun' begin to creep,
De little pickaninny's gone to sleep.

Mandy, w'at's de matter wid dat chile?
Keeps a-sighin' ev'y little w'ile;
Seems to me I heayhd him sorter groan,
Lord! his little han's am' col' as stone!
W'at's dat far-off light dat's in his eyes?
Dat's a light dey's borrow'd f'om de skies;
Fol' his little han's across his breas',
Let de little pickaninny res'.

[83]

THE RIVALS

Look heah! Is I evah tole you 'bout de curious
    way I won
Anna Liza? Say, I nevah? Well heah's how
    de thing wuz done.

Lize, you know, wuz mighty purty — dat's
    been forty yeahs ago —
'N 'cos to look at her dis minit, you might'n
    spose dat it wuz so.

She wuz jes de greates' 'traction in de county,
    'n bless de lam'!
Eveh darkey wuz a-co'tin, but it lay 'twix me
    an' Sam.

You know Sam. We both wuz wukin' on de ole
    John Tompkin's place.
'N evehbody wuz a-watchin' t'see who's gwine
    to win de race.

Hee! hee! hee! Now you mus' raley 'scuse me fu'
    dis snickering,
But I jes can't he'p f'om laffin' eveh time I tells
    dis thing.

Ez I wuz a-sayin', me an' Sam wuked daily side
    by side,
He a-studyin', me a-studyin', how to win Lize
    fu' a bride.

Well, de race was kinder equal, Lize wuz sorter
    on de fence;
Sam he had de mostes dollars, an' I had de mostes
    sense.

Things dey run along 'bout eben tel der come
    Big Meetin' day;
Sam den thought, to win Miss Liza, he had
    foun' de shoest way.

An' you talk about big meetin's!   None been
    like it 'fore nor sence;
Der wuz sich a crowd o' people dat we had to
    put up tents.

Der wuz preachers f'om de Eas', an' 'der wuz
    preachers f'om de Wes';
Folks had kilt mos' eveh chicken, an' wuz fat-
    tenin' up de res'.

Gals had all got new w'ite dresses, an' bought
    ribbens fu' der hair,
Fixin' fu' de openin' Sunday, prayin' dat de
    day'd be fair.

Dat de Reveren' Jasper Jones of Mount Moriah,
     it wuz 'low'd,
Wuz to preach de openin' sermon; so you know
     der wuz a crowd.

Fu' dat man wuz sho a preacher; had a voice
     jes like a bull;
So der ain't no use in sayin' dat de meetin' house
     wuz full.

Folks wuz der f'om Big Pine Hollow, some come
     'way f'om Muddy Creek,
Some come jes to stay fu' Sunday, but de crowd
     stay'd thoo de week.

Some come ridin' in top-buggies wid de w'eels
     all painted red,
Pulled by mules dat run like rabbits, each one
     tryin' to git ahead.

Othah po'rer folks come drivin' mules dat
     leaned up 'ginst de shaf',
Hitched to broke-down, creaky wagons dat
     looked like dey'd drap in half.

But de bigges' crowd come walkin', wid der new
     shoes on der backs;
'Scuse wuz dat dey couldn't weah em 'cause de
     heels wuz full o' tacks.

Fact is, it's a job for Job, a-trudgin' in de sun an'
      heat,
Down a long an' dusty clay road wid yo' shoes
      packed full o' feet.

'Cose dey stopt an' put dem shoes on w'en dey
      got mos' to de do';
Den dey had to grin an' bear it; dat tuk good
      religion sho.

But I mos' forgot ma story, — well at las' dat
      Sunday came
And it seemed dat evehbody, blin' an' deef, an'
      halt an' lame,

Wuz out in de grove a-waitin' fu' de meetin' to
      begin;
Ef dat crowd had got converted 'twould a been
      de end o' sin.

Lize wuz der in all her glory, purty ez a big sun-
      flowah,
I kin 'member how she looked jes same ez 'twuz
      dis ve'y houah.

But to make ma story shorter, w'ile we wuz
      a-waitin' der,
Down de road we spied a cloud o' dus' dat filled
      up all de air.

An' ez we kep' on a-lookin', out f'om 'mongst
    dat ve'y cloud,
Sam, on Marse John's big mule, Cæsar, rode
    right slam up in de crowd.

You jes oughtah seed dat darkey, 'clar I like
    tah loss ma bref;
Fu' to use a common 'spression, he wuz 'bout
    nigh dressed to def.

He had slipped to town dat Sat'day, didn't let
    nobody know,
An' had car'yd all his cash an' lef' it in de dry
    goods sto'.

He had on a bran' new suit o' sto'-bought clo'es,
    a high plug hat;
He looked 'zactly like a gen'man, tain't no use
    d'nyin' dat.

W'en he got down off dat mule an' bowed to
    Liza I could see
How she looked at him so 'dmirin', an' jes kinder
    glanced at me.

Den I know'd to win dat gal, I sho would need
    some othah means
'Sides a-hangin' 'round big meetin' in a suit o'
    homespun jeans.

W'en dey blow'd de ho'n fu' preachin', an' de
    crowd all went inside,
I jes felt ez doh I'd like tah go off in de woods
    an' hide.

So I stay'd outside de meetin', set'n underneat'
    de trees,
Seemed to me I sot der ages, wid ma elbows on
    ma knees.

W'en dey sung dat hymn, "Nobody knows de
    trouble dat I see,"
Seem'd to me dat dey wuz singin' eveh word o'
    it fu' me.

Jes how long I might ha' sot der, actin' like a
    cussed fool,
I don't know, but it jes happen'd dat I look'd
    an' saw Sam's mule.

An' de thought come slowly tricklin' thoo ma
    brain right der an' den,
Dat, perhaps, wid some persuasion, I could
    make dat mule ma fren'.

An' I jes kep' on a-thinkin', an' I kep' a-lookin'
    'roun',
Tel I spied two great big san' spurs right close
    by me on de groun'.

Well, I took dem spurs an' put em underneat' o'
    Cæsar's saddle,
So dey'd press down in his backbone soon ez
    Sam had got a-straddle.

'Twuz a pretty ticklish job, an' jes ez soon ez it
    wuz done,
I went back w'ere I wuz set'n fu' to wait an' see
    de fun.

Purty soon heah come de people, jes a-swa'min'
    out de do',
Talkin' 'bout de "pow'ful sermon" — "nevah
    heah'd de likes befo'."

How de "monahs fell convicted" jes de same
    ez lumps o' lead,
How dat some wuz still a-layin' same es if dey'd
    been struck dead.

An' to rectly heah come Liza, Sam a-strollin' by
    her side,
An' it seem'd to me dat darky's smile wuz 'bout
    twelve inches wide.

Look to me like he had swelled up to 'bout
    twice his natchul size,
An' I heah'd him say, "I'd like to be yo' 'scort
    to-night, Miss Lize."

Den he made a bow jes like he's gwine to make
    a speech in school,
An' walk'd jes ez proud ez Marse John over to
    untie his mule,

W'en Sam's foot fust touched de stirrup he
    know'd der wuz sump'n wrong;
'Cuz de mule begin to tremble an' to sorter side
    along.

W'en Sam raised his weight to mount him,
    Cæsar bristled up his ear,
W'en Sam sot down in de saddle, den dat mule
    cummenced to rear.

An' he reared an' pitched an' caper'd, only ez a
    mule kin pitch,
Tel he flung Sam clean f'om off him, landed him
    squar' in a ditch.

W'en dat darky riz, well raly, I felt kinder bad
    fu' him;
He had bust dem cheap sto' britches f'om de
    center to de rim.

All de plug hat dat wuz lef' him wuz de brim
    aroun' his neck,
Smear'd wid mud f'om top to bottom, well, he
    wuz a sight, I 'speck.

Wuz de folks a-laffin'? Well, su', I jes sholy
    thought dey'd bus';
Wuz Sam laffin'? 'Twuz de fus' time dat I
    evah heah'd him cuss.

W'ile Sam slink'd off thoo de backwoods I
    walk'd slowly home wid Lize,
W'en I axed her jes one question der wuz sump'n
    in her eyes

Made me know der wuz no need o' any answer
    bein' said,
An' I felt jes like de whole world wuz a-spinnin'
    'roun' ma head.

So I said, "Lize, w'en we marry, mus' I weah
    some sto'-bought clo'es?"
She says, "Jeans is good enough fu' any po'
    folks, heaben knows!"

If homely virtues draw from me a tune
In happy jingle or a half-sad croon;
Or if the smoldering future should inspire
My hand to strike the seer's prophetic lyre;
Or if injustice, brutishness and wrong
Should make a blasting trumpet of my song;
O God, give beauty and strength — truth to my
          words,
Oh, may they fall like sweetly cadenced chords,
Or burn like beacon fires from out the dark,
Or speed like arrows, swift and sure, to the mark.